MONTPELIER REGIONAL LIBRARY
RFD #2
MONTPELIER, VT. 05602

WITHDRAWN

PICK IT UP

by SAM and BERYL EPSTEIN

pictures by
TOMIE DE PAOLA

PICK IT UP

Holiday House • New York

Text copyright © 1971 by Sam and Beryl Epstein
Illustrations copyright © 1971 by Tomie de Paola
All rights reserved
Printed in the United States of America
Library of Congress catalog card number: 70-151759
ISBN 0-8234-0194-4

Do you pick up an apple and a marble in the same way? Try it and see.

Do you pick up the apple by grasping it between your thumb and your four other fingers and then lifting it?

Do you pick up the marble by grasping it between your thumb and one finger and then lifting it?

Are you picking up the apple and the marble in the same way? Yes, you are grasping each one before you lift it up.

Grasping is one way of getting hold of something. Whenever you pick up something, you must get hold of it before you can lift it.

How would you pick up this watermelon? Would you grasp it between both your hands and then lift it?

How would you pick up this big beach ball? Would you grasp it between your arms? If it is not too big, can you grasp it with one arm, by wrapping your arm around it?

Did you ever see an elephant grasp a log by wrapping his trunk around it? Did you ever see a monkey grasp a banana with his tail?

Can you think of a way to grasp something without using your hands or your arms?

Could you grasp an apple with your teeth? Try it.

Did you ever see a dog pick something up by grasping it with his teeth?

Did you ever see a bird pick up a worm by grasping it with his beak?

Can you think of any tools that pick up things by grasping them first?

This small pair of tongs can grasp a little cube of sugar. This big pair of tongs can grasp a big block of ice and make it easier to pick up.

This scientist uses tongs to pick up something he does not want to touch.

A pair of chopsticks grasps a piece of meat in the same way you grasp something between a thumb and a finger. Can you pick up something with a pair of chopsticks? Try it. You can use two long pencils for chopsticks.

This machine has a pair of metal jaws that close like teeth. It can grasp a huge rock and hold it. Then the rock can be lifted by the power of the machine's big engine.

What would be the best way to get hold of this shopping bag? Would you grasp it with your hands or your arms? Or would you curl your fingers around the handle?

When you curl your fingers you can use them as if they were a hook. Using a hook is another way to get hold of something.

This man is using a boat hook at the end of a long stick to pick up the hat he lost overboard.

Have you ever seen a wrecker pick up one end of a car? Did you see the hook that was used to get hold of the car?

When you pick up a piece of meat on a fork what are you doing? Are you grasping the meat? Are you hooking the meat? No, you are sticking the meat on the fork's sharp points.

Sticking or stabbing are other ways of getting hold of something to pick it up.

This man is getting hold of bits of paper by sticking them with the sharp point at the end of a stick.

This Eskimo is stabbing a fish with his spear through a hole in the ice.

How do you get hold of soup in order to pick it up? Do you grasp it or hook it or stick it? No. To pick up soup you use a spoon or some other kind of scoop.

Scooping is another way of getting hold of something to pick it up.

This cook is scooping up soup with a big spoon called a ladle.

This man is scooping up ice cream with a round ice cream scoop.

This boy is scooping up a pancake with a flat scoop called a spatula or a pancake-turner.

This girl is scooping up fish in a net.

The first astronaut on the moon used this special scoop to pick up rocks.

This man is picking up sand with a special machine called a loader. The machine scoops up the sand and lifts it by the power of its engine.

Do you know of any animals who get their food by scooping it up? A cat uses his tongue as a tiny scoop. The tongue picks up milk and carries it to the cat's mouth. A pelican has a big scoop on the lower part of his beak. With it he scoops small fish out of the water.

Can you make a scoop out of your hand? Try it. Hold your fingers close together and then bend them. You can scoop up sand with your hand. But if you try to scoop up water with your hand, some of the water will leak out between your fingers.

Can you think of any other way to pick up water? Could you suck it up through a straw?

Yes, sucking is another way of picking things up. When you drink soda through a straw, the soda flows upward into your mouth as you suck on the straw.

Did you ever see an insect suck up food? A bee sucks up tiny drops of honey from a flower. So does a butterfly. Does an elephant suck up water through his trunk?

Do you know about any machine that picks up things by sucking? A vacuum cleaner sucks up the dust on a rug. A water pump sucks up water from the ground.

Can you think of still another way to get hold of something so that you can pick it up?

Suppose your finger is sticky. And suppose you press your sticky finger on a crumb of bread. Will your sticky finger hold the crumb so that you can pick it up and put it into your mouth? Try it and see.

Can you think of any animal that picks up its food by using something sticky? An anteater has a very sticky tongue. He uses it to pick up the ants he likes to eat.

Do you know what this boy is doing? He has seen a coin under the metal grating. He cannot get his arm through the grating so that he can grasp the coin with his fingers. So he has tied a nail to a string, and stuck some sticky chewing gum to the nail.

He lowers the nail through the grating and lets the chewing gum touch the coin. The coin sticks to the chewing gum.

Now the boy has hold of the coin. All he has to do is lift it up by pulling the string.

Did you ever hear the saying:

> See a pin and pick it up.
> All the day you'll have good luck.

Can you think of a way to pick up a pin without touching it? You can pick it up with a magnet.
Hold the magnet close to the pin. The pin will jump to the magnet and cling to it.

You cannot pick up a piece of paper with a magnet, or a piece of wood. A magnet will pick up only things made of iron or steel. The power of a magnet to pick up iron and steel is called magnetism.

This huge magnet gets its magnetism from electricity. When the electricity is turned on the machine can lift this heavy load. When the electricity is turned off, it drops the load.

Can you think of a game that is played by picking things up?

This girl is playing the game of jacks. She bounces the ball. While the ball is in the air she tries to pick up the jacks.

These children are playing jackstraws. Jackstraws are tiny sticks of wood. A player hooks them up, one at a time, with a tiny hook at the end of a stick.

Can you think of any other games that are played by picking things up?

How many different ways of picking up things do you use in a day? Can you name the ways and count them?

Mark Zegri

About the Authors

Sam and Beryl Epstein have collaborated on many excellent books for children and young adults since their marriage in 1938.

Beryl Epstein was born in Ohio and received her undergraduate degree at Douglass College in New Jersey. Sam Epstein is a native of Boston and met his future wife in New Jersey where he attended Rutgers University.

The Epsteins now live and work in an old farmhouse on a salt inlet in Southold, Long Island, New York.

Frances McLaughlin—Gill

About the Artist

Tomie de Paola was born in Meriden, Connecticut. He received his B.F.A. from Pratt Institute in Brooklyn and in 1970 was granted a Ph.D. equivalency for his creative work at Lone Mountain College in San Francisco.

The author and artist of several children's books, he has illustrated many others. Two of his books were chosen by the American Institute of Graphic Arts (AIGA) as outstanding children's books for 1969-70. One of them, WHO NEEDS HOLES? was done in collaboration with the Epsteins.

He now lives in a two hundred year old converted tavern in New Hampshire and spends most of his time writing and illustrating children's books.

j531
Epstein, S
 Pick it up

C.2
MRL

WITHDRAWN

State of Vermont
Department of Libraries
Midstate Regional Library
RFD #4
Montpelier, Vt. 05602

DATE DUE

W A S NOV 1987	S - 9 13/15/99			
V X MAR 88				
JA 29 '88 975				
Fe 19 '88 1491				
Ma 11 '88 1478				
S-51				

VERMONT DEPT. OF LIBRARIES
0 00 01 0458071 7

DEMCO 38-301